Someone Is Listening

In The Spirit

30 Days of INSPIRATION ©

Someone Is Listening

In The Spirit

—— 30 Days of ——
INSPIRATION ©

Kesha Nichols

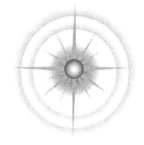

Unity In Spirit
Publishing

Someone Is Listening In The Spirit - 30 Days of Inspiration

Unless otherwise indicated, all Scripture quotations are taken from the King James Version of the Bible.

Scripture quotations marked AMP or Amplified are taken from THE AMPLIFIED BIBLE, as so indicated.

Someone Is Listening In The Spirit - 30 Days of Inspiration
ISBN 978-1-890201-03-6

Published by:
Unity In Spirit Publishing
P.O. Box 578
Austell, GA 30168
Phone: 770-948-2446
Fax: 770-948-2449

Printed in the United States of America

Table of Contents

Introduction

Someone Is Listening In The Spirit - 30 Days of Inspiration is not just your typical book on inspiration. Author Kesha Nichols has put her heart and soul into making this book a life-changing experience for every reader. Created specifically to inspire each and every person who reads it, *Someone Is Listening In The Spirit* will speak to the lives of many, bringing about the desire for a truly transformed life.

As the title of her book indicates, Ms. Nichols sees each of us as a spiritual being, living through human experiences, crying out in the spirit for the wisdom of life. To this end, God has an answer for us all.

> *I hear the cries of the spirit*
> *And while you are yet speaking . . .*
> *I am listening!*

As a parallel to life, this book presents us with many of life's challenges. In response to these challenges, *Someone Is Listening In The Spirit* . . . provides us with 30 days of devotions through the scriptural Word of God, which in turn becomes our source and foundation for moving into the place that God has called for each of us. In addition to the daily writings, Ms. Nichols challenges us to explore what lies within our spirit, by providing thought-provoking insights and questions through the use of 30 daily inspirations. These inspirations will allow you to search yourself, thereby taking the first step to growth and healing.

Finally, we have provided a personal reflections section at the end of each day to allow you to take the time to reflect upon your life and create your own personal journal. Through this 30-day process, *Someone Is Listening In The Spirit - 30 Days of Inspiration*, invites you to accept the challenge to renew and rejuvenate your life.

As you read the daily devotionals embodied in *Someone Is Listening In The Spirit - 30 Days of Inspiration*, it is Ms. Nichols' desire that you replenish your well of life, as you prepare yourself for a life-changing experience.

Remember, before you even call, He will answer and while you are yet speaking, He hears!

Someone Is Listening In The Spirit . . .

About the Author

Author and Motivator, Kesha Nichols is a native of New York. Born in Staten Island, she spent the first 24 years of her life in the city of New York. At the age of 24, her family relocated to Decatur, Georgia, where she currently resides.

Kesha credits this untimely move to the greater Atlanta area, as a catalyst to unveiling her destiny in life. She began to put her God-given talents and gifts to use through the form of expressive writing. Writing since the age of seven, her true talent for the written word began to manifest at the tender young age of eleven.

During the course of her spiritual and natural maturity, Kesha's writings have continued to elevate to new levels of understanding and inspiration. Her writings reflect the heart and soul of people everywhere, bringing forth written expression to that which many only feel. However, feelings are simply not enough, as the heart of mankind longs for wisdom, understanding, and knowledge. Her writings have been destined to become affirmations to one's soul, as they bring about life-changing transformations.

Ms. Nichols gives thanks to God for her life's experiences, both good and bad, as they have strengthened her resolve and opened her heart to a deeper understanding of life.

Dedication

This book is dedicated to my beloved aunt,
Gwendolyn Ann Norris,
who died tragically as a victim of domestic violence.

Domestic violence is a growing epidemic that touches the lives of men, women, children and families across our nation and throughout the world. It is perpetuated by acts of violent behavior by a person who is often intimately connected or in close relationship to the victim. Domestic violence is displayed through physical, psychological or sexual abuse and may even escalate to the point of death, as was the case with my Aunt Gwendolyn.

It is my goal to lend a hand in an effort to put an end to this epidemic of violence. As such, I pray that the words of this book will somehow reach those in need who are suffering from domestic violence, as well as those who perpetuate it, by serving to help encourage and renew their spirits.

I also pledge my support to this cause by donating a portion of the proceeds from these books to shelters and support groups focused on the eradication of domestic violence. I would like to thank each and every one of you for your support of this effort. Together, we can change lives.

Let's send a message loud and clear:

Someone Is Listening In The Spirit . . .

Acknowledgements

I would like to personally and publicly thank the following individuals, who have supported me wholeheartedly in the fulfillment of this vision.

LISA GADSON

Thank you for the long and often frustrating hours that you put into this project, oftentimes into the wee hours of the night. As a covenant partner, you have always been willing and able to serve.

FAMILY & FRIENDS

Showers of blessings to you all for your many encouraging words, financial support and simply believing that I COULD! I thank God that each of you has stayed close enough to share in the manifestation of this great vision.

TO EACH OF YOU

I would like to personally thank each and every one of you for allowing me the opportunity to share these words of inspiration with you. It is my prayer that the writings of this book, will bring about an awesome change in your life.

Preface

My desire for you as you read this book is to challenge you to open your spirit to be transformed, as the goodness of God saturates your being through the understanding and knowledge of His Word.

As you read through the daily words of inspiration, I want to inspire you to move beyond the place which you presently are and know that there is abundant life waiting after each situation we encounter in life. I want you to know that I believe in the power of the human spirit to restore and rejuvenate itself through wisdom, understanding and divine direction.

It is my heart's desire to be used in such a way that my own trials, tribulations, valleys and wilderness experiences have not been in vain, but can be used as a tool or instrument of inspiration for others.

On a daily basis, I have often asked myself this question, "Kesha, does it really matter that you are alive?" After reading this book, if you begin to be transformed and ultimately become all that you were called by God to be, you will have answered my question and brought assurance that it really does matter that I have lived and am alive today to share my thoughts and testimony of life. It is truly my God-ordained purpose to motivate and encourage God's people. It has been my humble pleasure to work on this book, the first of a twelve part series of books that are destined to propel you into a transformed and pleasurable life.

In His Service,

Kesha Nichols

Day 1

A New Beginning

Day 1

A New Beginning

> Brethren, I count not myself to have apprehended: but this one
> thing I do, forgetting those things which are behind
> and reaching forth unto those things which are before,
>
> I press toward the mark for the prize
> of the high calling of God in Christ Jesus.
> *Philippians 3:13-14*

A new day, a new beginning, a fresh start, another season of life to be lived! Today! YES, this very day is a perfect time to start anew and allow the power of God to rejuvenate your spirit to yet another level of being.

As the Apostle Paul states, he doesn't pretend or assume that he has reached the ultimate place of growth in his life, but the ONE thing that he does stake a claim to is the decision to forget those things which are BEHIND him.

We all know what THINGS Paul is referring to - the things that can make us doubt ourselves and God; the things that can cause us to stand still and not reach for our goals; the things that can bring trials and tribulations into our lives.

In this time of new beginnings, let's set our hearts to do as Paul did and begin to *"press toward the mark of the high calling."* Take this day to dream and visualize that, which is to come. Set obtainable goals and encourage yourself to strive to receive all that God has prepared for you.

Day 1

Inspiration

IDENTIFY: Today, make a conscious effort to forget those things which are behind you and turn each and every care into the hands of Christ. Write down all the negative things in your life you need to forget and leave behind.

_____

_____

_____

LOCATE: What do you consider to be the "*PRIZE of the high calling*" of God for your life?

_____

_____

_____

An EXERCISE in FAITH: What are you prepared to do in order to PRESS toward the MARK? What goals will you set for yourself that will lead you into the manifestation of God's will for your life?

_____

_____

_____

Day 1

Personal Reflections

_____

_____

_____

_____

_____

_____

_____

_____

_____

_____

_____

_____

_____

_____

_____

_____

_____

_____

_____

Day 2

*Mustard Seed
Faith*

Day 2

Mustard Seed Faith

> And Jesus said unto them, *Because of your unbelief: for verily I say unto you, If ye have faith as a grain of mustard seed, ye shall say unto this mountain, Remove hence to yonder place; and it shall remove; and nothing shall be impossible unto you.*
> Matthew 17:20

*F*or our God said, that if we have faith the size of a mustard seed, that we could speak to the mountains in our lives and command them to be removed by the power of God.

It is important to note, that Jesus chose to use the analogy of the mustard seed to demonstrate our faith. The mustard seed is one of the smallest of natural herbs, yet when planted in fertile soil, it grows up to be one of the strongest of all herbs.

According to Jesus, such is our faith. Like the natural process of the mustard seed, we must learn to spiritually apply mustard seed faith against every attack of the enemy. The Word of God tells us that with faith like a grain of mustard seed, we possess the unlimited power of God, which is able to defeat our enemies.

Begin today to speak to the mountains in your life and watch the awesome power of God move against every spiritual, emotional, and physical challenge that tries to hinder you.

Remember, FAITH like a grain of mustard seed - **NOW THAT'S FAITH!**

Day 2

Inspiration

IDENTIFY: Take the time to identify three mountains that exist in your life today.

_____

_____

_____

LOCATE: By faith, what are three promises that you are believing God for?

_____

_____

_____

An EXERCISE in FAITH: Using three mustard seeds, each representing your faith, place each seed in a special place, whether it be in your bible, under your pillow, or even in a garden. Pray consistently about your faith and watch as God begins to move on your behalf. Be sure to record God's answers to your prayers.

_____

_____

_____

Day 2

Personal Reflections

_____
_____
_____
_____
_____
_____
_____
_____
_____
_____
_____
_____
_____
_____
_____
_____
_____
_____
_____

Day 3

Think on These Things

Day 3

Think on These Things

> Finally, brethren, whatsoever things are *true*, whatsoever things are *honest*, whatsoever things are *just*, whatsoever things are *pure*, whatsoever things are *lovely*, whatsoever things are of a *good report*; if there be any *virtue*, and if there be any *praise*, think on these things.
> Philippians 4:8

VIRTUE: moral excellence, goodness, righteousness - conforming one's life to moral and ethical principals of a good or admirable quality with the inherent power to produce positive effects.

PRAISE: the expression of approval or admiration, commendation, the offering of grateful homage in word or song as an act of worship to God.

If there be any virtue or praise, we are to think upon the positive attributes that are essential to living a victorious Christian life. Truth, honesty, justice, purity, loveliness, a good report, virtue and praise are the makings of an enriched life.

Living an enriched life begins with the renewing of your mind and the expression of a positive YOU! Begin to feed yourself with a positive outlook on life - think the best even in the midst of your trials and tribulations.

Focus on the good in everyone and in every situation that you encounter. We have the power to frame our lives by the choices and decisions that we make, by the attitude we portray to others and by the representation of Christ in our lives.

Day 3

Inspiration

IDENTIFY: Focus on three areas in your life where you desire to initiate a positive change.

_____

_____

_____

LOCATE: Name three promises from the Word of God that will become your foundation for positive thinking.

_____

_____

_____

An EXERCISE in FAITH: Name three people who will be inspired by the positive change in your life. How will the glory of God in your life and the effects of your renewed spirit affect these people?

_____

_____

_____

_____

Day 3

Personal Reflections

_____
_____
_____
_____
_____
_____
_____
_____
_____
_____
_____
_____
_____
_____
_____
_____
_____
_____
_____

Day 4

The Bread of Life

Day 4

The Bread of Life

Then Jesus declared,
"I am the bread of life." *He who comes to me will never go hungry,*
and he who believes in me will never be thirsty.
John 6:35

*W*hen we think of "bread" in the natural, we often think of a fresh loaf of bread, one used to create an awesome sandwich or a compliment to a delicious entrée. In times past, many people looked forward to eating a slice of their Grandmother's homemade bread.

However, this "bread" as referenced in **John 6:35** is "bread" of a totally different nature. This "bread" is the "Bread of Life" through Christ Jesus.

As we previously discussed, natural bread is often eaten as nourishment for our health and natural bodies. However, as Christians, what has God chosen as the provision for our spirit, soul and body? It is the living, breathing spirit of the Almighty God that nourishes and sustains us in our Christian walk.

The word of God, as declared by Jesus boldly proclaims
"I am the Bread of Life."

As our spiritual provider, Jesus Christ is our all in all. He should be everything that we need, want or desire. He is that life sustaining power, a river of living water, and a source that never runs dry. The word tells us that we will neither hunger nor thirst if we come to and believe in Jesus Christ.

Partake of JESUS, the Bread of Life!

14

Day 4

Inspiration

IDENTIFY: As your personal "Bread of Life", in what areas do you need Christ to sustain you?

_____

_____

_____

LOCATE: What changes are you willing to make in order for God to be the great "*I AM*" in your life?

_____

_____

_____

An EXERCISE in FAITH: As an exercise, try to go for one week without eating natural bread of any kind. As the days go by, you may find it extremely hard to refrain and you will eventually have a desire to eat bread again. Likewise, if we try to live without Christ in our lives, we will eventually reach a point of surrender, where we will need Christ, like the need for daily bread. Just imagine living without Christ in your life.

By faith, what steps will you make to receive your daily bread?

_____

_____

Day 4

Personal Reflections

_____

_____

_____

_____

_____

_____

_____

_____

_____

_____

_____

_____

_____

_____

_____

_____

_____

_____

_____

_____

Day 5

Celebrate Life!

Day 5

Celebrate Life!

This is the day the Lord has made,
let us be glad in it.
Psalm 118:25

*W*e are admonished by the word of God to *rejoice* and be glad in the wonder of God's creation. Just imagine, God created a whole day, 24 hours just for us to enjoy.

No matter what may come your way, *REJOICE* and again I say *REJOICE*! God has handcrafted this very day and every one after it, with His divine intention that we should *rejoice* and be glad in it. We owe it to ourselves to receive this precious gift of God's anointing and take dominion over each and every day of our lives.

Begin to celebrate life as if it was the first day of the rest of your life. Live life to the fullest, as if it was your last day here on earth. We owe it to ourselves to live each day as God has ordained, with joy and gladness.

Whatever brings you joy, seek to infuse your life with the elements of joy. Whether it's going out to dinner to your favorite restaurant, spending time with family and friends, or simply pampering yourself with quiet solitude, *REJOICE*! Whether you are going fishing or sitting by the lake with a good book, enjoy each and everyday of your life. Whatever makes you happy; determine in your heart that you will seek after the joy of the Lord.

AND AGAIN I SAY *REJOICE*!

Day 5

Inspiration

IDENTIFY: Today, I will encourage myself to celebrate life by:

_____

_____

_____

LOCATE: All around us there are people who do not see life from the perspective of *Psalms 118:25*. Find someone who has not realized God's abundant grace and begin to encourage them to rejoice over life as God has commanded. *(Even if that someone is you.)*

God, today I will encourage:

_____

_____

_____

An EXERCISE in FAITH: As a testimony to the change God has made in your life, start a daily log by keeping a record of all the areas in your life that have given you a reason to celebrate.

_____

_____

_____

Day 5

Personal Reflections

_____

_____

_____

_____

_____

_____

_____

_____

_____

_____

_____

_____

_____

_____

_____

_____

_____

_____

_____

_____

_____

_____

_____

Day 6

Because I Am Holy

Day 6

Because I Am Holy

> I am the Lord who brought you up out of Egypt to be your God,
> therefore be holy, because I am holy.
> *Leviticus 11:45*

*T*he promises of God to this present generation are the same promises He has made to His people from generation to generation. The promise to take them out of their "Egypt" situations and become their God.

No matter what your Egypt situation may be, God is able to deliver. His only request is that we allow Him to enter into our lives, and that we live holy. Why?

Because He Is Holy

How often have you heard that still, small voice speaking clearly to your spirit saying,

Take my hand whenever you fall,
for I will pick you up.
Call out to me when you are lost
and I will show you the way.
When sickness tries to overtake you,
simply reach out and touch the hem
of My garment and I will make you whole.

This is the voice of the Lord speaking to your spirit saying,

"I am God and I will supply your every need,
if you just trust in me."

Day 6

Inspiration

IDENTIFY: Take the time to identify the Egypt situations in your life, then seek God's face for your deliverance.

_____

_____

_____

LOCATE: Deliverance is a mighty experience and one worthy of our praise. Locate areas in your life that once represented an Egypt situation. Begin to praise God for your deliverance!

_____

_____

_____

An EXERCISE in FAITH: After identifying your Egypt situation, what steps are you taking in order to walk out of Egypt?

_____

_____

_____

Day 6

Personal Reflections

_____

_____

_____

_____

_____

_____

_____

_____

_____

_____

_____

_____

_____

_____

_____

_____

_____

_____

_____

_____

_____

_____

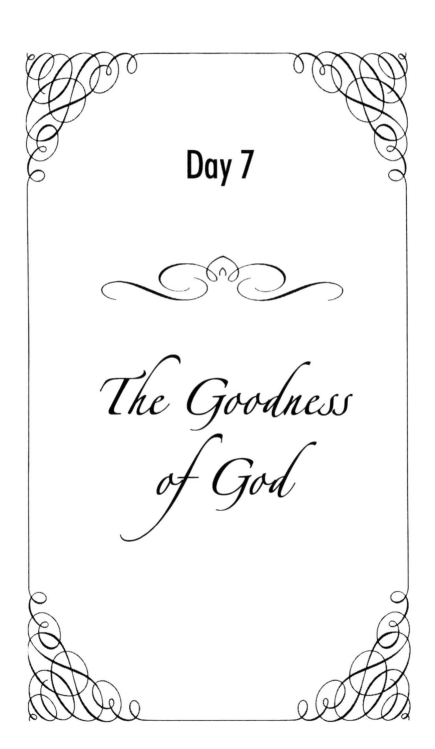

Day 7

The Goodness of God

Day 7

The Goodness of God

> And the Lord said, *I will cause all my goodness to pass in front of you, and I will proclaim my name, the Lord in your presence. I will have mercy on whom I will have mercy, and I will have compassion on whom I will have compassion.*
> Exodus 33:19

The goodness of the Lord has gone before you. His goodness and His mercy have paved the way for your life to spring forth. He has given us all of His goodness, nothing left out, nothing held back. In your very presence, the Lord has proclaimed Himself to be the source of all that is good and meaningful in life. By His own word, He has chosen to show mercy and compassion upon those He chooses.

Isn't this a wonderful thing to be covered in the mercy and compassion of the Father? Many will attest to the fact that before great success, there was the experience of failure; and before true peace there were the overwhelming trials of confusion and disruption. However, when the Lord saw fit to show His mercy and compassion through grace, He ultimately revealed His perfected will.

Through His will of mercy and compassion, know the true goodness of God.

Day 7

Inspiration

IDENTIFY: Can you determine a point in your life when the mercy and compassion of God was undeniably evident in your life?

_____

_____

_____

LOCATE: When you find yourself dealing with a particular situation in life and become uncertain as to its outcome, remember the goodness of God, shown through His mercy and compassion. In these types of situations I will always:

_____

_____

_____

An EXERCISE in FAITH: God's goodness has passed before me, in honor of God, I will:

_____

_____

_____

Day 7

Personal Reflections

_____

_____

_____

_____

_____

_____

_____

_____

_____

_____

_____

_____

_____

_____

_____

_____

_____

_____

_____

_____

_____

_____

Day 8

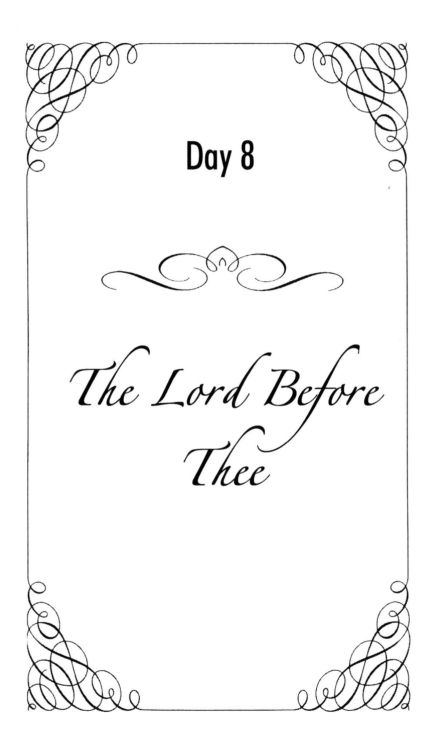

The Lord Before Thee

Day 8

The Lord Before Thee

> And the Lord, He it is that doth go before thee;
> He will be with thee, He will not fail thee, Neither forsake thee:
> fear not, neither be dismayed.
> *Deuteronomy 31:8*

$\mathcal{T}$he above scripture makes a profound statement regarding the responsibility of the Lord towards us. Just in case we ever find ourselves not understanding the role the Lord serves in our lives, this scripture reminds us:

It is He that . . .

"Goes before thee" - The Lord will lead and guide us into all truth.

"He will be with thee" - The Lord will always be with us. We can rest assured that we can abide in His Holy presence.

"He will not fail thee" - You can trust and depend on the Lord. Unlike man, He will keep His promises and never fail you.

"He will neither forsake thee" - As He has promised throughout His word, He will never leave us, or forsake us.

"Fear not, neither be dismayed" - In the presence of the Lord, we can stand bold and courageous, living each day without fear.

In Christ, we live, we move and we have our being.

Day 8

Inspiration

IDENTIFY: In order for the Lord to go before you, you must first submit to His lordship and grant Him authority over your life. In order for the Lord to go before you, what areas of your life are you willing to submit to his authority?

_____

_____

_____

LOCATE: Knowing that the Lord will go before you, what are you willing to do to ensure God's presence in your life?

_____

_____

_____

An EXERCISE in FAITH: What must you do in order to live a life that is without fear and free from the cares of this world?

_____

_____

_____

Day 8

Personal Reflections

_____

_____

_____

_____

_____

_____

_____

_____

_____

_____

_____

_____

_____

_____

_____

_____

_____

_____

_____

Day 9

If You Only Knew

Day 9

If You Only Knew

> But as it is written, eye hath not seen, nor ear heard, neither have entered into the heart of man, the things which God hath prepared for them that love Him.
> But God hath revealed them unto us by His Spirit, for the Spirit searcheth all things, yea, the deep things of God.
> *I Corinthians 2:9-10*

"Eye hath not seen" - We have not even begun to comprehend the full manifestation of God's desire for our lives.

"Nor ear heard" - We often speak of our desire to live our lives in the perfect will of God. However, our ears have not yet heard the manifold wisdom of God's plans and purposes, as it relates to each of us.

"Neither have entered into the heart of man" - We have only scratched the surface of understanding the desires of our hearts, as it relates to God.

The good news is that God has revealed all these things to us by His Spirit. If we strive to live our lives by the Spirit of God, we will live in harmony with God's perfect will and all things will be made known to us. The Spirit searches out even the deepest things of God and reveals them to us for our good.

Day 9

Inspiration

IDENTIFY: As God reveals His vision for your life, begin to paint a picture in your mind's eye of the many plans He has in store for you. As referenced in the scripture, Habakkuk 2:2, take some time to write down your vision and make it plain.

_____

_____

_____

LOCATE: God has a way of speaking volumes of peace and promise into our lives through His word. What promises have been revealed to you by God's Spirit?

_____

_____

_____

An EXERCISE in FAITH: What are the desires of your heart? What will you determine in your heart to do, in order for your desires to be manifested?

_____

_____

_____

Day 9

Personal Reflections

_____

_____

_____

_____

_____

_____

_____

_____

_____

_____

_____

_____

_____

_____

_____

_____

_____

_____

_____

_____

Day 10

Reclaim Your

Peace

Day 10

Reclaim Your Peace

> Peace I leave with you, my peace I give unto you;
> not as the world giveth, give I unto you.
> Let not your heart be troubled, neither let it be afraid.
> John 14:27

*T*hese are the words spoken by Jesus to His people with a lasting promise that will span from generation to generation. His expression of peace brings forth words of encouragement spoken to a wrestling heart; words of power spoken to the weak; and words of tranquility spoken in the midst of utter confusion.

PEACE
MY PEACE - I GIVE UNTO YOU

These are the words of Jehovah God, spoken through His anointed one; the messenger of great tidings, the Bearer of Peace.

In this world you will have trials, yet, He has promised us unending peace. Not the false sense of peace that the world tries to serve us on tarnished platters, but the true peace of God in all of its quiet calm and gentle serenity.

The time has come to reclaim your peace! Shut the door to confusion, lock out the spirit of chaos, worry and defeat and reclaim the wonderful gift of peace.

Day 10

Inspiration

IDENTIFY: What issues in your life have become barriers to your peace?

_____

_____

_____

LOCATE: What specific steps do you need to initiate in order to reclaim the peace that God has promised to you?

_____

_____

_____

An EXERCISE in FAITH: I make a conscious effort to maintain a high level of peace in my life. I will start by:

_____

_____

_____

_____

Day 10

Personal Reflections

Day 11

With a Heart of Thanksgiving

Day 11

With a Heart of Thanksgiving

> Offer unto God thanksgiving;
> and pay thy vows unto the Most High.
> *Psalm 50:14*

*W*ith a heart full of thanksgiving, rejoice in the glory and majesty of our Lord. I admonish you to become continually thankful for that which you already have, as you praise God for the many blessings that are yet to come.

Giving thanks to God is our responsible duty and is honorable in the sight of God. He honors our prayers and abides in our praise of thanksgiving. Rejoice in the Lord daily and witness His enduring goodness and mercy upon our lives.

God will honor His word to continually bless our lives when we demonstrate our gratefulness in even the little things in life. It is truly a blessing and a reason for thanksgiving to simply exist and abide in God's grace.

With a heart full of the joy of the Lord, offer unto God thanksgivings and strive to keep and fulfill your vows unto the Lord, Most High.

Day 11

Inspiration

IDENTIFY: There are so many things in life for which we should be thankful. Examine your life and recognize the areas in your life where you are most thankful.

_____

_____

_____

LOCATE: Take the time right now to thank God for something that may seem small or insignificant to others, yet vital and important to your life.

_____

_____

_____

An EXERCISE in FAITH: In response to God's faithfulness to us, we are also required to be faithful to Him. Whenever we make a vow unto God or a heartfelt promise, we should endeavor to keep our vows. What vow or promise to God do you need to uphold?

_____

_____

_____

Day 11

Personal Reflections

_____

_____

_____

_____

_____

_____

_____

_____

_____

_____

_____

_____

_____

_____

_____

_____

_____

_____

_____

Day 12

Arise and Shine

Day 12

Arise and Shine

> ARISE, SHINE; for thy light is come,
> and the glory of the Lord is risen upon thee.
> *Isaiah 60:1*

*A*rise and Shine for the light that fuels our lives is the glory of the Lord God Almighty, rising upon each and every one of us. It is by this light that we live and have our being.

If we strive to allow His light *(His Power, His Presence, His Peace)* to engulf our lives, it will fuel a fire from deep within that will shine so brightly, as to illuminate the pathway of our lives.

Whether we are weathering through the storms of life or find ourselves at the point of seemingly total darkness, our light will somehow find a way to shine through it all. For the light of life that shines so deeply within us cannot be destroyed by any situation or circumstance we encounter in life.

We each possess a torch of the Holy Light of Life; so let your light shine before mankind, yielding a breath of light to the pathway of others who may need our guidance.

I am put in remembrance of the words of an old spiritual that states, "This little light of mine, I'm going to let it shine . . ."

I encourage you today - ARISE and SHINE!

Day 12

Inspiration

IDENTIFY: What areas of your life need to be illuminated by the Light of Life?

_____

_____

_____

LOCATE: In what area of your life does your light shine most brightly?

_____

_____

_____

An EXERCISE in FAITH: What can you do to spread God's power, His peace and His presence in the lives of others? Identify ways in which you can share your life with someone who may be living in darkness.

_____

_____

_____

_____

_____

Day 12

Personal Reflections

_____

_____

_____

_____

_____

_____

_____

_____

_____

_____

_____

_____

_____

_____

_____

_____

_____

_____

_____

_____

_____

_____

Day 13

Looking Ahead

Day 13

Looking Ahead

> Behold, the former things are come to pass, and new things do I
> declare: before they spring forth I tell you of them.
> *Isaiah 42:9*

*M*ake a conscious effort to let go of the former things in life, or those things that represent your broken past. Don't allow yourself to look back on experiences, situations or circumstances that can serve as stumbling blocks, keeping you from moving forward toward your future.

When we focus on what is behind us, we cannot possibly see what is ahead. It is similar to driving a car down a busy highway, looking through the rear view mirror - eventually you will crash.

You are on your way to God's appointed destiny, which is directly before you, yet you continue to look back on your life at the mistakes you have made or the disappointments you may have experienced. If you choose to remain in the past, you literally place your spirit in a stagnant place where God is not free to move in your life.

The only real purpose for briefly reflecting on your past is to remind you to rejoice over where God has brought you from, as you set your focus on where God is taking you.

Day 13

Inspiration

IDENTIFY: Have you truly taken the time to allow the former things to pass from your life? What have you decided to leave behind?

_____

_____

_____

LOCATE: How can looking back hinder you from moving forward?

_____

_____

_____

An EXERCISE in FAITH: The Lord said that as the former things pass away, He would declare new things to spring forth in our lives. What new thing has God ordained to spring forth in your life?

_____

_____

_____

_____

_____

Day 13

Personal Reflections

_____

_____

_____

_____

_____

_____

_____

_____

_____

_____

_____

_____

_____

_____

_____

_____

_____

_____

_____

_____

_____

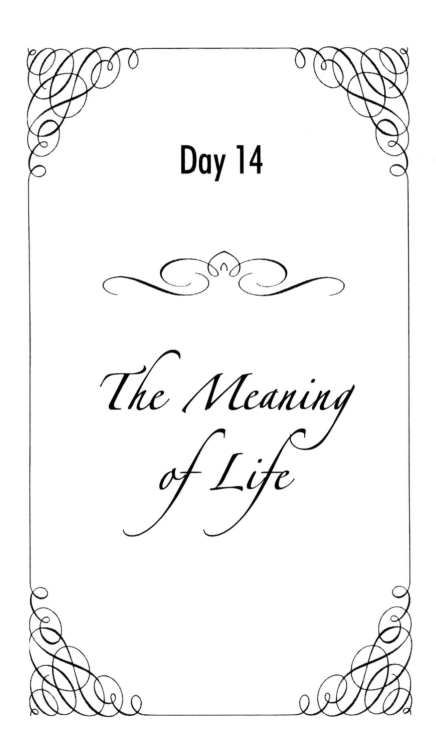

Day 14

The Meaning of Life

Day 14

The Meaning of Life

So I commend the enjoyment of life, because nothing is better
for a man under the sun than to eat and drink
and be glad then joy will accompany him in his work
all the days of the life God has given him under the sun.
Ecclesiastes 8:15

LIFE IS:

A SONG ~ Sing it with joy and rejoice before the Lord.

A MYSTERY ~ Destined to unfold. Abide in the presence of the Lord and He will reveal all that He has hidden for us.

A JOURNEY ~ Prepare for it and walk it out with endurance.

WONDERFUL ~ Enjoy the sheer splendor of it all and embrace each and every precious moment.

PRECIOUS ~ Determine not to waste a single moment or abuse the time God has given.

A GIFT ~ Unwrap the Master's gift for the whole world to see.

UNLIMITED ~ Go for it; do not be hindered by man-made boundaries or limitations.

LIGHT ~ Let your life shine so brightly before men that they may glorify the God that is in you.

LOVE ~ For God so loved the world, He gave us his only begotten son.

LIFE IS ALL THIS AND MORE!

Day 14

Inspiration

IDENTIFY: Take the time to examine what LIFE really means to you. Write a love letter to God, sharing the intimacy of your heart and the gratitude you feel towards Him.

_____

_____

_____

LOCATE: Starting this very moment, what changes will you make to enhance the quality of your life?

_____

_____

_____

An EXERCISE in FAITH: Life is such a precious gift from God. What impact can you have on the life of a child or young adult who is currently in your life? I will impact change by:

_____

_____

_____

Day 14

Personal Reflections

_____
_____
_____
_____
_____
_____
_____
_____
_____
_____
_____
_____
_____
_____
_____
_____
_____
_____
_____
_____

Day 15

My Rock
and
My Fortress

Day 15

My Rock and My Fortress

> Bow down thine ear to me: deliver me speedily: be thou my strong rock, for an house of defense to save me.
> For thou art my rock and my fortress; therefore for thy name's sake lead me and guide me. Pull me out of the net that they have laid privily for me, for thou art my strength.
> *Psalm 31:2-4*

*I*t's time to let go of the things that bind you and allow yourself to be lead by the Spirit of the Lord. God is indeed our rock and our fortress, a mighty covering for us in our time of need.

You may find yourself in a wilderness situation, in a state of despair or even experiencing the darkest moment in your life. However, I want to encourage you that God is there. He can and will see you through, if you would only trust in Him.

Open up your spirit and allow Him to freely move within you. Allow the Spirit to lead you and God will empower you to have a successful journey. Even in the midst of the experiences of life's many trials and tribulations, never forget that God is with you always.

Walk in the Spirit and know that God has inclined His ear to heed your every call. He will deliver you speedily, for He is your strength.

Day 15

Inspiration

IDENTIFY: Determine in your heart that no matter what you go through, you will call on the name of the Lord. What areas in your life do you currently need God's guidance in?

_____

_____

_____

LOCATE: Today's lesson was entitled "*My Rock and My Fortress.*" Can you remember a time in your life when the Lord was a rock and a fortress, supporting you through the trials of life?

_____

_____

_____

An EXERCISE in FAITH: Share this encouraging word with others. Who do you know that is in need of a spiritual place of refuge?

_____

_____

_____

Day 15

Personal Reflections

_____

_____

_____

_____

_____

_____

_____

_____

_____

_____

_____

_____

_____

_____

_____

_____

_____

_____

_____

_____

Day 16

Prepare for Life's Trials

Day 16

Prepare For Life's Trials

> Consider it pure joy, whenever you face trials of many kinds,
> because you know that the testing of your faith
> develops perseverance.
> *James 1:2*

*W*ho would have thought that the trials of life could bring about joy? It seems absurd to even think that something bad could bring about something good. However, in God's system, we know that all things work together for the good of them that love the Lord.

Oftentimes, when we reach the end of a problem or situation in life, we want to believe that it is finished and that surely, nothing else could possibly happen. Certainly, life should not confront us with yet another situation or circumstance, especially since the last one took us to the doorstep of hell and back. Sometimes life seems so unfair, but we must remember that God is sovereign and we do not always understand the challenges with which we are faced.

What we do know is that according to the scriptures, the testing of our faith develops our spiritual character and perseverance. So the next time that you are faced with the trials of life - count it all joy. Look at your situation head on and proclaim yourself to be more than a conqueror! Know that each situation in life prepares us for that which is to come.

Day 16

Inspiration

IDENTIFY: Recognizing that we are constantly in a mode of spiritual preparation, what lessons have you learned from past trials or tribulations.

_____

_____

_____

LOCATE: Remembering the last victory in your life, how did that situation strengthen your character and personally enhance you?

_____

_____

_____

An EXERCISE in FAITH: What trial of life are you currently dealing with? What natural and spiritual strategies will you put in place to guarantee your victory?

_____

_____

_____

Day 16

Personal Reflections

_____

_____

_____

_____

_____

_____

_____

_____

_____

_____

_____

_____

_____

_____

_____

_____

_____

_____

_____

_____

_____

Day 17

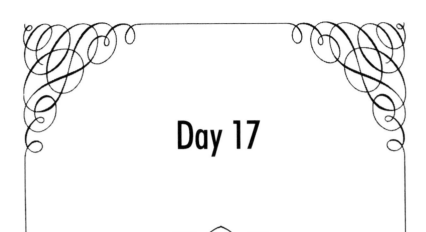

In Everything
Give Thanks

Day 17

In Everything Give Thanks

> Rejoice ever more. Pray without ceasing. In everything give thanks:
> for this is the will of God in Christ Jesus concerning you.
> *I Thessalonians 5:16-18*

*Y*ou may not have everything that you want, but you do have everything that you need. The needful thing is to know that you have an advocate with the Father, who will supply all of your needs according to His riches in glory in Christ Jesus. So basically, you do have what you need and in Christ you have everything.

When we begin to focus on worldly things, we need only shift our thinking over to spiritual matters. For instance, you may not have a lot of money in the bank, yet on a spiritual level, your heavenly Father has wealth beyond measure stored up just for you. You may not live in a large or stately home, however your heavenly Father has many mansions and He has prepared a place for you.

I want to encourage you to realize, that the mere fact that you are alive, breathing and operating out of a sound mind, your needs are being met and you have more than enough.

Rejoice over what you have, pray to the Father without ceasing and give thanks continually for everything and in all things. In everything give thanks, for this is indeed the will of God in Christ Jesus concerning you and I.

Day 17

Inspiration

IDENTIFY: Looking over my life, I find that I am truly thankful for the following:

_____

_____

_____

LOCATE: What have you determined to be the will of God for your life?

_____

_____

_____

An EXERCISE in FAITH: In your present situation, everything may not seem to be functioning, as it should. However, in the midst of it all, can you find one area where God deserves the glory?

_____

_____

_____

_____

Day 17

Personal Reflections

_____

_____

_____

_____

_____

_____

_____

_____

_____

_____

_____

_____

_____

_____

_____

_____

_____

_____

_____

_____

Day 18

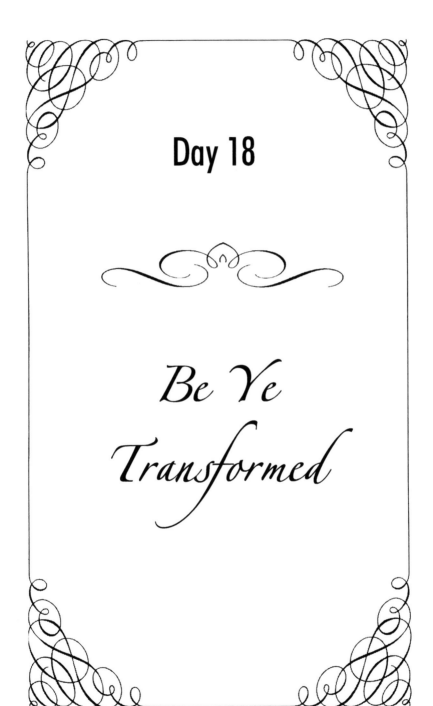

Be Ye Transformed

Day 18

Be Ye Transformed

> And be not conformed to this world: but be ye transformed by the renewing of your mind, that ye may prove what is that good, and acceptable, and perfect will of God.
> *Romans 12:2*

*L*iving in this world system, we are often pressured to conform our lives and our character to the ways of the world. The environment, in which we live, undoubtedly has great impact and influence over our lives. No matter how the world seeks to conform us, we must realize that in Christ, there is a higher standard.

This elevated standard of living can only be realized when we each begin to renew our minds to embrace the plans and purposes of God. ***Romans 12:2*** admonishes us not to be ruled, governed, changed or conformed to this present world. The wonderful thing about God's Word is that it always offers an alternative. The scripture strongly requests that we transform ourselves by the powerful act of renewing our minds. Renewal of the mind comes about by simply changing the way we think, which in turn will change the way we react.

By setting your mind to think on the good and acceptable will of God, you will in essence change your entire life! God has empowered each and every one of us with the spirit of power and of a sound mind. God's empowerment allows us to live in this world, without becoming subject to or bound by its ways.

Day 18

Inspiration

IDENTIFY: I will begin immediately to transform my life. The first thing that I will do is:

_____

_____

_____

LOCATE: Take the time to examine your life. Are there any areas in your life that you feel you may have conformed to the world's way?

_____

_____

_____

An EXERCISE in FAITH: I believe that God's good and perfect will for my life includes the following:

_____

_____

_____

_____

_____

Day 18

Personal Reflections

Day 19

One Accord
One Mind

Day 19

One Accord - One Mind

> If there be therefore any consolation in Christ, if any comfort of love, if any fellowship of the Spirit, if any bowels and mercies,
>
> Fulfill ye my joy, that ye be likeminded, having the same love, being of one accord, of one mind.
> *Philippians 2:1-2*

*W*hatever your situation in life may be, allow Christ to console and comfort you. Christ's request for us to become likeminded supports His desire that we be on one accord and operating out of one mind, the "Mind of Christ".

Being of one mind with Christ, sets your life on course with His desires. We take comfort in knowing that He loves us and that His mercy towards us endures forever. Fellowship in the Spirit, and allow Christ to move you to an elevated state of mind. Peace, love, joy and prosperity will be the by-products of your fellowship with Christ. Allowing yourself to be led by the Spirit will guide you effortlessly into the place of your destiny.

Your inner spirit has the power to deliver you from the trials of life and any challenges that the adversary may place before you. Being on one accord and likeminded with Christ is the foundation on which we can boldly stand with confidence.

Day 19

Inspiration

IDENTIFY: We each desire to be on one accord with Christ. What issues or concerns do you need to address in order to have the mind of Christ?

_____

_____

_____

LOCATE: Reflect on a time when you had to seek the comfort and counsel of God. What life lessons did you learn?

_____

_____

_____

An EXERCISE in FAITH: In the same spirit that we strive to be on one accord with Christ, it is also the fulfillment of His joy that we seek the same in our relationships with others. What can you do to be more like Christ and be on one accord with individuals in your life?

_____

_____

_____

Day 19

Personal Reflections

_____

_____

_____

_____

_____

_____

_____

_____

_____

_____

_____

_____

_____

_____

_____

_____

_____

_____

_____

_____

_____

Day 20

Treasure

of

The Heart

Day 20

Treasure of The Heart

> For where your treasure is, there will your heart be also.
> *Luke 12:34*

*Y*our heart holds the key to your destiny. It is the place chosen by God to hold the treasures of life. The heart of man secures the intimacy of the secrets that God has spoken regarding your very life. It is the site of your deepest wants and desires; for all that you are is manifested within the heart.

At all cost, the word of God admonishes us to guard our hearts. It is imperative that we maintain a strong heart, for a strong heart is healthy and fertile ground on which God can bring forth His perfect will. Keep your heart free of life's burdens, sadness, anxiety, stress and fear.

Alleviate the weight of grief and despair, keeping your heart and soul free to receive the many treasures that God has prepared for you. Clean out the treasurer chest of your heart, allowing God the opportunity to freely give you all things. Remember, a pure heart is an open window to heaven.

Day 20

Inspiration

IDENTIFY: If God were to examine the contents of your heart, what would He find there?

_____

_____

_____

LOCATE: What issues of life have you allowed to burden your heart?

_____

_____

_____

An EXERCISE in FAITH: Name one negative thing that may be taking up precious space in your heart.

_____

_____

_____

_____

_____

Day 20

Personal Reflections

Day 21

The Spirit of Hope

Day 21

The Spirit of Hope

> For I know the thoughts that I think toward you,
> saith the Lord, thoughts of peace and not of evil,
> to give you (hope) for an expected end.
> *Jeremiah 29:11*

$\mathcal{T}$he Lord has set His thoughts towards us. Our needs, wants and desires are at the forefront of His mind. It is a blessing of the heart to know that the Lord is mindful of us.

His thoughts toward us are merciful, thoughts of good and not of evil. Whatever the Lord thinks, so shall it be established. Who can challenge the mind of Christ towards us? Our peace is in knowing that the Lord is ever mindful of us. It brings great HOPE to even the most challenged spirit to know that the Lord is on our side. Set your HOPE upon the Lord and He will establish your expected end.

HOPE is making the impossible . . . POSSIBLE
HOPE is making the unbelievable . . . BELIEVABLE
HOPE is making the unseen . . . SEEN
HOPE will always keep you focused on . . . YOUR FUTURE
HOPE embraces the reality of greater possibilities for . . . TOMORROW

True joy comes from the Lord. Set your heart to seek after His perfect will and He will reveal His plans to you. As the scriptures indicate, His thoughts include plans of peace, prosperity and HOPE for an expected end.

Day 21

Inspiration

IDENTIFY: The Spirit of Hope is knowing that Christ is ever mindful of us. What thoughts has the Lord revealed to your spirit?

_____

_____

_____

LOCATE: Knowing that God has a good and expected end for your life, what are three things you believe God will manifest in your life?

_____

_____

_____

An EXERCISE in FAITH: HOPE has a way of keeping our minds focused on the future. What has God set in place for your future?

_____

_____

_____

_____

_____

Day 21

Personal Reflections

_____

_____

_____

_____

_____

_____

_____

_____

_____

_____

_____

_____

_____

_____

_____

_____

_____

_____

_____

_____

Day 22

*These Things
I Have Spoken*

Day 22

These Things I Have Spoken

> These things I have spoken unto you that in me ye might have peace.
> In the world ye shall have tribulations: but be of good cheer;
> I have overcome the world.
> *John 16:33*

*D*o not be weary when faced with the challenges and obstacles of life. Always remember, when we are weak, He is yet strong. Always believe that there lies great strength in our time of weakness, for God is our ever-present source of strength. It is important to recognize the spirit of defeat. However, we must be mindful not to be overcome by it. Keep allowing righteous energy to navigate your path in life and accept the strength He allows to support your victory over defeat.

With a renewed outlook that emphasizes the healing in spiritual strength, we can rejoice and proclaim the goodness of God's promise. When it is all said and done, we can all be of good cheer, for He (Christ) has overcome the world.

Day 22

Inspiration

IDENTIFY: In what areas of your life do you currently feel weak? Call on the name of the Lord for your strength.

_____

_____

_____

LOCATE: Name three areas where God has given you strength.

_____

_____

_____

An EXERCISE in FAITH: Be mindful to avoid the spirit of defeat. In order to avoid becoming defeated, I will:

_____

_____

_____

_____

_____

Day 22

Personal Reflections

_____

_____

_____

_____

_____

_____

_____

_____

_____

_____

_____

_____

_____

_____

_____

_____

_____

_____

_____

Day 23

Your Future Awaits

Day 23

Arise and Shine

> Howbeit when He, the Spirit of Truth, is come,
> He will guide you into all truth: for He shall not speak of himself;
> but whatsoever He shall hear, that shall He speak,
> and He will show you things to come.
> *John 16:13*

*Y*our future is not determined by your present condition. Neither is it restricted by your past. Before the foundations of the earth, God spoke your destiny into being, while you were not yet formed in your mother's womb. The very essence of God was placed on the inside of you, for you hold all power within you.

Our divine spirit and every single act of unshakeable faith has the power to guide us onto the pathway of our destiny. When the Spirit of Truth abides on the inside of us, He is able to guide us into all truth concerning our lives. God will reveal to you hidden treasures in secret places, which He has preordained for your life here on earth.

Keep the faith, seek God and allow the Spirit to guide you to your destiny.

Day 23

Inspiration

IDENTIFY: The Spirit of Truth speaks directly from the heart of God into our spirit. What is God speaking to your spirit?

_____

_____

_____

LOCATE: Being led by the Spirit, I wholeheartedly expect a promising future, to include:

_____

_____

_____

An EXERCISE in FAITH: What great things have been revealed to you about your purpose in life?

_____

_____

_____

_____

Day 23

Personal Reflections

Day 24

It Begins Within

Day 24

It Begins Within

> Now the God of hope fill you with all joy and peace in believing,
> that ye may abound in hope, through the power of the Holy Ghost.
> *Romans 15:13*

*T*he happiness, peace and joy you are searching for begins and ends within you. Each and every morning give yourself a dose of self-therapy.

Look at yourself in the mirror and declare out loud -

Peace is mine! Happiness is mine! Joy is mine!

Say this over and over again until your spirit is saturated with the power of the Holy Ghost. Make it a daily habit to edify and encourage yourself. Begin to speak into existence those things you desire. Speaking those things that may not quite exist, as though they do, by faith. Go ahead - begin NOW!

As you declare the beauty of God's hand over your life, begin to thank God for His many blessings. TODAY, your day has already been set. It's a GREAT day, even before you step out of your front door!

Day 24

Inspiration

IDENTIFY: What constitutes peace, happiness and joy for you?

_____

_____

_____

LOCATE: For the enhancement of your life, what character traits has God groomed on the inside of you that need to come forth?

_____

_____

_____

An EXERCISE in FAITH: Today, I will edify and encourage myself by:

_____

_____

_____

_____

_____

Day 24

Personal Reflections

_____

_____

_____

_____

_____

_____

_____

_____

_____

_____

_____

_____

_____

_____

_____

_____

_____

_____

_____

Day 25

Yesterday, Today
&
Tomorrow

Day 25

Yesterday, Today & Tomorrow

> The Lord your God hath multiplied you, and behold, ye are this day
> as the stars of heaven for multitude.
> The Lord God of your fathers make you a thousand times
> so many more as ye are, and bless you, as he hath promised you.
> *Deuteronomy 1:10-11*

*B*ehold the promises of God are upon you. God in His infinite wisdom and grace has promised through His word to multiply you, as the stars in the heaven above.

YESTERDAY'S trials and tribulations are no more, as they are yet vapors in the sea of forgotten memories.

TODAY is your opportunity to take God at His word, rebuking the challenges of life, as you open your heart to receive His manifested blessings.

TOMORROW holds the essence of God's promise that the best is truly yet to come.

Wherever you are in life, God has promised through His word to guide you through.

Day 25

Inspiration

Taking God at His word, we can each look into our lives and see the many manifested promises of God. Taking the time to take inventory of your Yesterday, Today and Tomorrow, you will find the strong hand of the Father moving on your behalf.

YESTERDAY God did . . .

_____

_____

_____

TODAY God has . . .

_____

_____

_____

TOMORROW God will . . .

_____

_____

_____

Day 25

Personal Reflections

_____

_____

_____

_____

_____

_____

_____

_____

_____

_____

_____

_____

_____

_____

_____

_____

_____

_____

_____

_____

Day 26

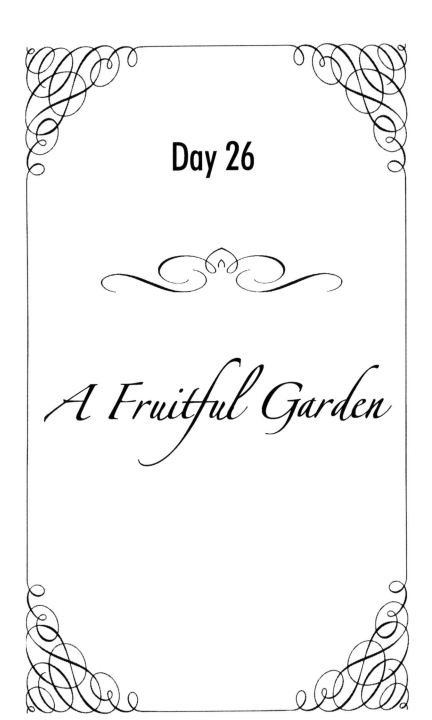

A Fruitful Garden

Day 26

A Fruitful Garden

> Be not deceived; God is not mocked:
> for whatsoever a man soweth, that shall he also reap.
> For he that soweth to his flesh shall of the flesh reap corruption;
> But he that soweth to the Spirit shall of the Spirit reap life everlasting.
> *Galatians 6:7-8*

*H*ow often have you heard the old adage: "*You Reap What You Sow*"? What this simply means is that like a farmer, whatever you plant (sow) will be what you will eventually harvest (reap).

Deuteronomy 22:9 sheds a biblical light on this same concept. Whatever seeds you determine to sow in your life will be representative of the fruit you can expect to harvest. Would you plant daisies in hopes of one day seeing vibrant red roses? Would you plant seeds of bitterness and hatred, yet expect to live a good and peaceful life?

Likewise, sowing seeds of poverty and lack will bring forth a harvest of mental, physical and financial insufficiency. Sowing seeds of lust, will bring forth unrighteous thoughts, which will in turn bring forth unrighteous actions that will eventually lead to addictive behaviors such as drug, alcohol and sexual immorality.

Make a decision today to begin to plant seeds of prosperity in your life. Determine in your heart that you will not defile your fruitful garden with the thorns of negativity. Always remember, it is a guaranteed fact, proven by the laws of life, that you will eventually reap what you sow.

Day 26

Inspiration

IDENTIFY: What positive seeds have you planted in your life and the lives of others?

_____

_____

_____

LOCATE: As you honestly reflect upon your life, determine which negative seeds you may have planted that warrant a full and undeniable "CROP FAILURE".

_____

_____

_____

An EXERCISE in FAITH: Acknowledging that you will eventually reap what you sow, what seeds will you make a responsible effort to sow?

_____

_____

_____

_____

Day 26

Personal Reflections

_____

_____

_____

_____

_____

_____

_____

_____

_____

_____

_____

_____

_____

_____

_____

_____

_____

_____

_____

_____

_____

Day 27

*Rejoice
In Yourself*

Day 27

Rejoice In Yourself

> But let every man prove his own work, and then shall he have rejoicing in himself alone, and not in another.
> *Galatians 6:4*

*Y*ou are magnificently crafted by the hand of God, created in His likeness and His image. There is no one with the exact same attributes as you. You have been uniquely made for the fulfillment of God's preordained purpose.

God created you with such great pride, dignity, confidence, self-respect and amazing beauty. This is truly a reason to rejoice.

Take the time to stop and admire the handiwork of the Father. Admire the structural elegance of your stature, the chiseled beauty of your character and the breathtaking light of your spirit as it shines forth into the lives of others. There are so many reasons to rejoice.

When God completed His craftsmanship in you, He sat down, put up His feet, folded His arms behind His head and said ...

~WELL DONE~

Day 27

Inspiration

IDENTIFY: Today, I will rejoice in myself. I will start by:

_____

_____

_____

LOCATE: Let's do a character analysis. What attributes of your character are you most pleased with?

_____

_____

_____

An EXERCISE in FAITH: If there are any areas in your life that are not as pleasing to you, what effort will you make to groom yourself into the perfect will of God?

_____

_____

_____

_____

Day 27

Personal Reflections

_____

_____

_____

_____

_____

_____

_____

_____

_____

_____

_____

_____

_____

_____

_____

_____

_____

_____

Day 28

Like Parent
Like Child

Day 28

Like Parent - Like Child

> Only take heed to thyself, and keep thy soul diligently,
> lest thou forget the things which thine eyes have seen,
> and lest they depart from thy heart all the days of thy life;
> but teach them thy sons, and thy son's sons.
> *Deuteronomy 4:9*

*P*arents, raise your children in a Godly fashion, living your life daily as an example before them.

If you want your child to maintain their virginity until marriage,
Set the Example . . . Don't commit fornication.

If you want your child to be God-fearing,
Set the Example . . . Fear God, teach them to live Godly and share the true principals of life, as found in the Word of God.

If you want your child to receive a good education,
Set the Example . . . Maintain an active role in their education, attend parent/teacher meetings and set them on the pathway of success.

If you want your child to be responsible,
Set the Example . . . Be responsible and hold them accountable for their deeds and actions.

As Christ showed us through His obedience to the Father - *Become a living, breathing example.*

Day 28

Inspiration

IDENTIFY: What example are you setting for the youth in your life?

_____

_____

_____

LOCATE: If asked, what positive comment would a child have to say about you?

_____

_____

_____

An EXERCISE in FAITH: As it relates to today's topic, "*Like Parent - Like Child,*" what life lessons have you learned from God the Father?

_____

_____

_____

_____

Day 28

Personal Reflections

_____

_____

_____

_____

_____

_____

_____

_____

_____

_____

_____

_____

_____

_____

_____

_____

_____

_____

Day 29

It's All Good

Day 29

It's All Good

> Observe and hear all these words which I command thee, that it may go
> well with thee and with thy children after thee forever, when thou doest
> that which is good and right in the sight of the Lord thy God.
> *Deuteronomy 12:28*

*D*oing what is good, right and proper in the sight of the Lord always has its good and just reward. Hold onto all that is good, wonderful, great and beautiful in your life, so that you will be a living, breathing example of God's righteousness.

Set yourself as a vessel of honor, an instrument of praise and a banner of righteousness for all to see. Observing to do what is commanded of us of the Lord, we will be a living legacy to our children and our children's children for generations to come.

Philippians 4:8 tells us whatever things are true, honest, just, pure, lovely and of a good report, we are to think on these things. These are the very things that develop the attributes of a positive spirit.

Those who come in contact with you will be overshadowed by the goodness of the Lord within you. Strive daily to be that source of God's goodness in the earth.

Day 29

Inspiration

IDENTIFY: In what ways do you express the goodness of God to others?

_____

_____

_____

LOCATE: Take some time to examine yourself - what good attributes do you see in yourself?

_____

_____

_____

An EXERCISE in FAITH: By doing what is right in the sight of the Lord, what example are you setting for others?

_____

_____

_____

_____

Day 29

Personal Reflections

Day 30

*You
And Only You*

Day 30

You And Only You

> For thou art a holy people unto the Lord thy God; the Lord thy God
> hath chosen thee to be a special people unto himself, above all
> people that are upon the face of the earth.
> *Deuteronomy 7:6*

*W*e are a holy people unto God. He has chosen us and set us aside for His divine and special purpose. Those who God has chosen for His purpose, man cannot deny or denounce.

You are that special someone, chosen of God for His purpose. You are a unique individual with style and attributes all your own. No two people exist that share the same blueprint of life or even the same calling or mission to be fulfilled. You were created for His purpose.

You and only you can fulfill the call of God for your life. There is something so very specific that has been written on the scrolls of time that you and only you can fulfill. Your mother can't do it, your best friend can't do it, not even your mate can do it - ONLY YOU!

It should be an honor and a pleasure to go before God and seek out His perfect will for your life. Spend some quality time in the secret place with Him and simply ask:

Father, what will you have me to do?
What was your plan for my life when you created me
from the foundations of this world?

Once he answers, be quick to obey. Only you can do it.

Day 30

Inspiration

IDENTIFY: Have you ever taken the time to ask God what His purpose is for your life? If so, what did he say?

_____

_____

_____

LOCATE: What do you consider to be your individual style and attributes? How do you use them to benefit yourself and others?

_____

_____

_____

An EXERCISE in FAITH: Isn't it time to fulfill your life's purpose? What can you do today to place yourself on your road to destiny?

_____

_____

_____

_____

Day 30

Personal Reflections

_____

_____

_____

_____

_____

_____

_____

_____

_____

_____

_____

_____

_____

_____

_____

_____

_____

_____

From the Publisher's Desk

As the Publisher of Unity In Spirit Publishing, I am truly privileged to have had the opportunity to work on this delightfully inspiring devotional. *Someone Is Listening In The Spirit - 30 Days of Inspiration*, has definitely been an inspiration to my spirit.

I am honored to be one of the very first to be inspired by its sound scriptural foundation, heartfelt inspiration, and thought-provoking insight. I am a firm believer that lives can truly be transformed through the gentle, encouraging words shared in the writings of this gifted author, Ms. Kesha Nichols.

Ms. Nichols has done an excellent job of searching the hearts of God's people, to give written expression to the very issues we all experience in our daily lives. Ms. Nichols has taken the time to reveal to us the answers to these many issues, by allowing her heart to hear from God through His spirit.

Come and share in this life-changing experience, as these words of life leap from the pages, in an effort to transform your life. On behalf of my staff and I, we pray God's wisdom, understanding and knowledge be yours now and forever.

As it is written,
Someone Is Listening In The Spirit

Karen M. Atkins
Publisher

We pray that the content and the character of this publication
has been a blessing to you. We look forward to hearing your comments.

SPIRIT 2 SPIRIT
Enterprises

Kesha Nichols
Spirit 2 Spirit Enterprise, LLC
P.O. Box 11802
Atlanta, GA 30355
s2senterprise@aol.com / s2senterprise.com
404-284-3203

Unity In Spirit
Publishing

Karen M. Atkins
Unity In Spirit Publishing
P.O. Box 578
Austell, GA 30168
unitynspir@aol.com / unity-n-spirit.com
770-948-2446 Phone / 815-377-2071 eFax

Publication Order Form

SOMEONE IS LISTENING IN THE SPIRIT
30 Days of Inspiration

We would like to thank you for your interest in *Someone Is Listening In The Spirit - 30 Days of Inspiration*. We pray that you have been blessed by this publication and have a desire to share it with others.

Additional copies of this book may be ordered by simply completing the attached order form and mailing it to the address listed below or by contacting Unity In Spirit Publishing at 770-948-2446.

Name: _____

Address: _____

City: _____

State: _____ Zip: _____

Credit/Debit Card#: _____

❏ American Express ❏ Discover ❏ MasterCard ❏ Visa

❏ Check ❏ Money Order

Product	Quantity	Amount	Subtotal
Someone Is Listening In The Spirit - *30 Days of Inspiration*		$12.95	
Shipping & Handling ($2.50 each publication)		$2.50	
		TOTAL	

Unity In Spirit Publishing
"Where Visions Become Reality"
P.O. Box 578, Austell, GA 30168
770-948-2446 Office
770-948-2449 Fax • 815-377-2071 eFax